World Picture
ATLAS

Holly Wallace

QEB
QEB Publishing

Published in the United States by
QEB Publishing, Inc.
3 Wrigley, Suite A
Irvine, CA 92618

www.qeb-publishing.com

A CIP record for this book is available
from the Library of Congress.

Printed and bound in Singapore

ISBN 978 1 59566 744 1

Author Holly Wallace
Consultants Clive Carpenter and
   Terry Jennings
Editor Eve Marleau
Designer Lisa Peacock
Cartography Red Lion

Publisher Steve Evans
Creative Director Zeta Davies
Managing Editor Amanda Askew

The words in *bold italic* are explained in the glossary on page 46.

Picture credits

Key: t=top, b=bottom, r=right, l=left, c=center,
PP=People and Places, PR=Products and Resources,
PA=Plants and Animals

8–9 PP: Shutterstock 9tl Richard Welter, 9tr Maridav, 9c Konstantin Shevtsov, 9bl Jim Guy, 9bc Anson Hung, 9br Taylor Jackson PR: Shutterstock 9tl Petr Vaclavek, 9tr Tatiana Edrenkina, 9cl Dalibor, 9cr Jovan Nikolic, 9b Lorraine Swanson PA: Shutterstock 8tl Mike Tan C.T, 8tc psamtik, 8tr Atlaspix, 8bl Scarabaeus, 8bc Chas, 8br Viacheslav V. Fedorov
10–11 PP: Shutterstock 11tl Mike Norton, 11tc Sandra van der Steen, 11tr Iofoto, 11cl Chee-Onn Leong, 11cr IPK Photography, 11b Bhathaway PR: Shutterstock 11tl ArchMan, 11tr Chepe Nicoli, 11cl MaszaS, 11cc Charles T. Bennett, 11cr Nikola Bilicb, 11b Jovan Nikolic
PA: Shutterstock 10tl Steve Byland, 10tc Eric Isselée, 10tr Ultrashock, 10bl Mighty Sequoia Studio, 10bc Kippy Lanker, 10br
12–13 PP: Shutterstock 12t Jennifer Scheer, 12cl Stuart Monk, 12cc Lisa F. Young, 12cr Albo, 12bl Condor 36, 12br Rob Byron PR: Shutterstock 13tl Gnuskin Petr, 13tc Jiri Vaclavek, 13tr Nikola Bilic, 13cl Christopher Dodge, 13cr Anat-oli, 13b Heidi Brand
PA: Shutterstock 13tl James Pierce, 13tc Gabor Ruff, 13tr A Cotton Photo, 13bl Goldenangel, 13bc R, 13br Mike Truchon
14–15 PP: Corbis 15cl Roger Ressmeyer Shutterstock 15t RJ Lerich, 15ccl Scott Kapich, 15ccr RJ Lerich, 15cr Timothy Lee Lantgen, 15b Slazdi PR: Shutterstock 15tl Ahnhuynh, 15tcl ShutterVision, 15tcr Provasilich, 15tr Sean Gladwell, 15bl Marcel Jancovic, 15br Geoffrey Kuchera PA: Photoshot 14tr NHPA/Lee Dalton Shutterstock 14tl Joseph Galea, 14tc Vitaly Romanovich, 14cl Eric Isselée, 14bl Jaana Piira, 14br Eky Chan
16–17 PP: Alamy Images 16tl Peter Arnold Inc/ Arnold Newman, 16b Moodboard Shutterstock 16tc ATesevich, 16tr Guentermanaus, 16cr Ostill, 16cl Grigory Kubatyan PR: Shutterstock 17tl Matka Wariatka, 17tr Heidi Brand, 17cl Ronald Sumners, 17cr Tatiana Edrenkina, 17bl Pavelr, 17br TsR PA: Shutterstock 17tl Karen Givens, 17tr Urosr, 17cl Graeme Knox, 17cc ZTS, 17cr Rubens Alarcon, 17b

Eric Gevaert
18–19 PP: Shutterstock 18tl Urosr, 18tc Misha Shiyanov, 18tr Pablo H Caridad, 18cl Mausinda, 18cr Dan Breckwoldt, 18b Damian Gil PR: Alamy Images 19cr Arco Images GmbH Photolibrary 19tl National Geographic Shutterstock 19tr Susan L. Pettitt, 19cl Eric Isselée, 19cc ClimberJAK, 19b Eric Isselée
PA: Shutterstock 19tl Marcel Jancovic, 19tr CG-Art, 19cl Filipe B. Varela, 19cc Nikola Bilic, 19cr Eric Isselée, 19b Daniel Kirkegaard Mouritsen
20–21 PP: Alamy Images 21cl ZenZimage Shutterstock 21tl Bond Girl, 21tr WitR, 21cc Eric Gevaert, 21cr Aneta Skoczewska PR: Shutterstock 21tl Heidi Brand, 21tr Pennyimages, 21cl Rui Vale de Sousa, 21cc Fotohunter, 21cr Shira Raz, 21b Odelia Cohen
PA: Dreamstime 20tl Shutterstock 20tc Gert Johannes Jacobus Vrey, 20tr Tezzstock, 20bl Christian Musat, 20bc Bill Kennedy, 20br Arkady
22–23 PP: Shutterstock 23tl Ostill, 23tr Lukas Hlavac, 23cl Alessio Ponti, 23cc Galyna Andrushko, 23cr Faberfoto, 23b Enote PR: Alamy Images 23tl Blickwinkel Shutterstock 23tr James Steidl, 23cl Nathalie Dulex, 23cc Riekephotos, 23cr Norman Chan, 23b Vinicius Tupinamba PA: FLPA 22bl Michael & Patricia Fogden Shutterstock 22tl Liga Alksne, 22tcl Eric Isselée, 22tcr Victor Soares, 22tr Jenny Horne, 22br Helder Almeida
24–25 PP: Shutterstock 25t Stefanie van der Vinden, 25cl Michael Jung, 25cc PhotoSky 4t com, 25cr Sculpies, 25bl Pichugin Dmitry, 25br Lucian Coman
PR: Shutterstock 25tl Amfoto, 25tc Daniel Kirkegaard Mouritsen, 25tr Teresa Azevedo, 25bl, 25bc Johnny Lye, 25br Ahnhuynh PA: Shutterstock 24tl Graeme Shannon, 24tr Johan Swanepoel, 24cl Mashe, 24cc Eric Isselée, 24cr David Thyberg, 24b NREY
26–27 PP: Alamy Images 27tr Robert Harding Picture Library Ltd Getty Images 27cr Denis Charlet/AFP Shutterstock 27tl Joe Gough, 27cl Igor Kisselev, 27cb Stephen Finn, 27b Stelian Ion PR: Corbis 26bl Niall Benvie ©2004 The LEGO Group 27tr Shutterstock 27tl Tatiana Edrenkina, 27tr Tyler Olson, 27bc, 27br Falk Kienas PA: Shutterstock 26tl Eric Isselée, 26tc Stephen Finn, 26tr Keith Levit, 26cl HTuller, 26cr Thomas O'Neil, 26b 3355m
28–29 PP: Shutterstock 29tl Mary Lane, 29tc Vladimir

Sazonov, 29tr Nagy Melinda, 29cl Alexey Arkhipov, 29cr Senai Aksoy, 29b Cristina Ciochina PR: Shutterstock 28tl Vladimir Chernyanskiy, 29tr János Németh, 28cl Prono Filippo, 28cr Zuzule, 28bl Scodaru, 28br Tatarszkij PA: Shutterstock 29tl Nikola Bilic, 29tr Gallimaufry, 29cl Sspopov, 29cr Dima Kalinin, 29bl Tund, 29br Yuliyan Velchev
30–31 PP: Shutterstock 30tl Piotr Bieniecki, 30tc PixAchi, 30tr Gueorgui Ianakiev, 30cl Sergey Kamshylin, 30cr Brykaylo Yuriy, 30b Brent Wong PR: Shutterstock 31tl Arteretum, 31tr Eric Isselée, 31cl Eric Isselée, 31cc Berit Ullmann, 31cr ARTSILENSEcom, 31b Steve Noakes PA: Getty Images 31tl De Agostini Picture Library Shutterstock 31tr Ilker Canikligil, 31cl Alekcey, 31cc Katja Kodba, 31cr Blazej Maksym, 31b Dinadesign
32–33 PP: Alamy Images 33b Bryan & Cherry Alexander Photography Shutterstock 33tl Alexander Chelmodeev, 33tc Denis Babenko, 33tr Dmitry Kosterev, 33cl Scodaru, 33cr Tatiana Grozetskaya PR: Rex Features 33b Shutterstock 33tl Sergey Petrov, 33tc Elena Schweitzer, 33tr Nicole Branan, 33bl Daniel G.Mata, 33bc Dalibor PA: Shutterstock 32tl Vladimir Melnik, 32tc Letty17, 32tr 3355m, 32bl Arnold John Labrentz, 32bc Tina Rencelj, 32br Eric Isselée
34–35 PP: Shutterstock 35tl Joseph Calev, 35tc Markus Sevcik, 35tr Chubykin Arkady, 35cl Ayazad, 35cr Connors Bros., 35b Vladyslav Byelov PR: Getty Images 35tl Lonely Planet Images/Patrick Syder Shutterstock 35tr Jovan Nikolic, 35cl Mircea Bezergheanu, 35cc Johannsen, 35cr Arteretum, 35b Losevsky Pavel PA: Alamy Images 34br Mike Lane Shutterstock 34tl Armin Rose, 34tc John A. Anderson, 34tr Debra James, 34bl Debra James, 34bc Seleznev Oleg
36–37 PP: Alamy Images 36tl Pal Teravagimov, 36tr Chris Howey, 36cl Lebedinski Vladislav, 36cr ARTEKI, 36cc Jeremy Richards, 36b 0399778584 PR: Shutterstock 37tl Robyn Mackenzie, 37tr Micha Rosenwirth, 37cl Ygrek, 37cr Arteretum, 37bl Marc Dietrich, 37br Norman Chan PA: Shutterstock 37tl Thorsten Rust, 37tr Karen Givens, 37cl Narcisa Floricica Buzlea, 37cc Benson HE, 37cr Irakite, 37b Vladimir Wrangel
38–39 PP: Alamy Images 39tr Mick Viet/Danita Delimont, 39tc Image Broker Shutterstock 39tl Lakis Fourouklas, 39cl Vlad Zharoff, 39cr David Wardhaugh,

39b Gusev Mikhail Evgenievich PR: Shutterstock 39tl Olga Lyubkin, 39tc Karen Winton, 39tr Joao Virissimo, 39bl A Schweitzer, 39br Jakub Kozák, 39bc Le Loft 1911 PA: Istockphoto 38br Chris Dascher Shutterstock 38tl Kkaplin, 38tr Stanislav Khrapov, 38cl Craig Dingle, 38cr David Mckee, 38bl Jeff Carpenter
40–41 PP: Alamy Images 41cl Dennis Cox Shutterstock 41tl Tan Kian Khoon, 41tc Craig Hanson, 41tr Mares Lucian, 41cr Holger Mette, 41b Freelion
PR: Shutterstock 41tl Norman Chan, 41tcl Gosper, 41tcr Grzym, 41tr E.G.Pors, 41bl Robyn Mackenzie, 41br Ivaschenko Roman PA: Alamy Images 40br Natural Visions/Heather Angel Shutterstock 40tl Eric Gevaert, 40tc Dmitrijs Mihejevs, 40tr Eric Isselée, 40bl J. Norman Reid, 40bc Shi Yali
42–43 PP: Alamy Images 43b David Wall Shutterstock 43tl Jose Gil, 43tr Vera Bogaerts, 43cl Brooke Whatnall, 43cc 4745052183, 43cr Midkhat Izmaylov PR: Shutterstock 43tl Luis Francisco Cordero, 43tc RTimages, 43tr Mitzy, 43bl Marylooo, 43bc Michael C. Gray, 43br Philip Lange PA: Alamy Images 42bc Stephen Frink Collection Shutterstock 42tl Olga Lyubkina, 42tc Jason Stitt, 42tr Susan Flashman, 42bl Martin Horsky, 42br Mark R Higgins
44–45 PP: Alamy Images 44cl Mediacolor's Shutterstock 44tl Viktor Gmyria, 44tr Chris Howey, 44cc Konstantin Shevtsov, 44cr Scott Kapich, 44b Armin Rose PR: Shutterstock 45tl HelleM, 45tr Vera Bogaerts, 45cl Ramona Heim, 45cc Tonylady, 45bl Alex0001, 45br Sam Chadwick PA: Shutterstock 44tl Nice_Pictures, 44tr Jan Martin Will, 44cl Ivan Histand, 44cr Gail Johnson, 44bl Popovici Loan, 44br Andromed

Contents

How to use this atlas

Maps are drawings of what the Earth looks like from above. Maps show important features such as deserts, rivers, and oceans, and how far apart countries are from each other in the world. A book of maps is called an *atlas*.

(1) Title
This tells you which part of the world the map shows.

(2) Locator globe
This shows where in the world the countries on the map are.

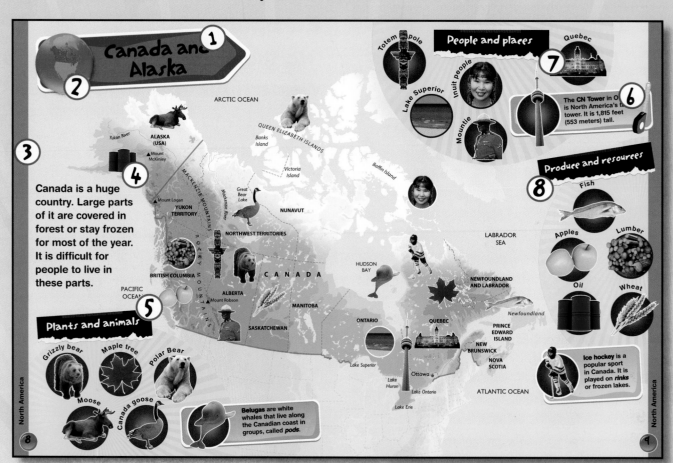

(3) Side panel
This is the name of the *continent* that the countries on the map are in.

(4) Picture
Every picture in the yellow bubbles is on the map. Can you find them all?

(5) Plants and animals
Many different kinds of plants and animals live all over the world.

(6) Scale
This means that this mountain, waterfall, or building is shown on the *scale* on page 5.

(7) People and places
The countries of the world and the people that live there can be different in many ways.

(8) Produce and resources
Countries grow, make, or use different things, such as oranges, cars and ice hockey, to make money.

What's on the map?

Maps use different kinds of writing and colors to show what is in each country. For example, a country name will look different than a river name. **Symbols** show features such as **capital cities**.

NORWAY	CANARY ISLANDS	Sonoran Desert	AHAGGAR MOUNTAINS
Country name	Territory	Desert	Mountain range
	Seram	*Lake Vänern*	ATLANTIC OCEAN
Country border	Island	Lake	Ocean
OHIO	*ARU ISLANDS*	*Missouri River*	BAY OF BISCAY
State	Group of islands	River	Small sea
	Berlin●	▲ Mount Galdhøpiggen	
State border	Capital city	Mountain	Ice

Color key

These colors show how high and how dry land is in different areas.

	more than 6,500 feet (2,000 meters)
	5,000–6,500 feet (1,500–2,000 meters)
	3,300–5,000 feet (1,000–1,500 meters)
	1,650–3,300 feet (500–1,000 meters)
	330–1,650 feet (100–500 meters)
	0–330 feet (0–100 meters)

Mount Everest is 29,029 feet (8,848 meters) high. That's the height of 16 CN Towers.

How high?

A scale can help to show the different sizes of mountains. If you see this symbol, come back to this page to see how big things really are.

The CN Tower is 1,814 feet (553 meters) tall. That's the height of 185 buses.

A bus is about 10 feet (3 meters) high.

Cotopaxi Volcano 19,350 feet (5,897 meters)
Mount Kilimanjaro 19,340 feet (5,895 meters)
Mount Elbrus 18,510 feet (5,642 meters)
Mount Ararat 16,833 feet (5,137 meters)
Mont Blanc 15,780 feet (4,810 meters)
Colima Volcano 14,206 feet (4,330 meters)
Mount Erebus 12,450 feet (3,795 meters)
Mount Fuji 12,388 feet (3,776 meters)
Mount Etna 10,922 feet (3,329 meters)

Mount Olympus 5,977 feet (2,919 meters)
Mount Pinatubo 4,872 feet (1,485 meters)
Table Mountain 3,563 feet (1,086 meters)
Mount Rushmore 3,537 feet (1,078 meters)
Angel Falls 3,212 feet (979 meters)

30,000 ft
28,000 ft
26,000 ft
24,000 ft
22,000 ft
20,000 ft
18,000 ft
16,000 ft
14,000 ft
12,000 ft
10,000 ft
8,000 ft
6,000 ft
4,000 ft
2,000 ft
0 ft

World map

The countries of the world are divided into seven continents, or areas. The continents are surrounded by *oceans*. The *Equator* is a line on maps that shows the middle of the Earth.

NORTH AMERICA

ATLANTIC OCEAN

PACIFIC OCEAN

EQUATOR

SOUTH AMERICA

North, south, east and west

A *compass* shows what direction north, south, east, and west are in. North and south point to the North and South poles. You can say "Naughty Elephants Squirt Water" to help you remember the directions.

N aughty

E lephants

S quirt

W ater

ARCTIC OCEAN

EUROPE

ASIA

AFRICA

PACIFIC OCEAN

EQUATOR

INDIAN
OCEAN

AUSTRALIA

SOUTHERN OCEAN

ANTARCTICA

Canada and Alaska

Canada is a huge country. Large parts of it are covered in forest or stay frozen for most of the year. It is difficult for people to live in these parts.

ARCTIC OCEAN

QUEEN ELIZABETH ISLANDS

Banks Island

Victoria Island

Yukon River

ALASKA (USA)

▲ Mount McKinley

▲ Mount Logan

YUKON TERRITORY

MACKENZIE MOUNTAINS

Mackenzie River

Great Bear Lake

NUNAVUT

NORTHWEST TERRITORIES

R O C K Y   M O U N T A I N S

BRITISH COLUMBIA

PACIFIC OCEAN

ALBERTA

▲ Mount Robson

C A N A D A

MANITOBA

SASKATCHEWAN

Plants and animals

Grizzly bear

Maple tree

Polar Bear

Moose

Canada goose

Belugas are white whales that live along the Canadian coast in groups, called *pods*.

Totem pole

Quebec

Lake Superior

Inuit people

Mountie

The CN Tower in Ontario is North America's tallest tower. It is 1,815 feet (553 meters) tall.

Produce and resources

Baffin Island

Fish

Apples

Lumber

LABRADOR SEA

HUDSON BAY

NEWFOUNDLAND AND LABRADOR

Newfoundland

Oil

Wheat

ONTARIO

QUEBEC

PRINCE EDWARD ISLAND

NEW BRUNSWICK

NOVA SCOTIA

Lake Superior

Ottawa

Lake Huron

Lake Ontario

Lake Erie

ATLANTIC OCEAN

Ice hockey is a popular sport in Canada. It is played on *rinks* or frozen lakes.

North America

9

Western USA

The United States of America, or the USA, is made up of 50 states, including Alaska (see page 8). The western states have everything from high mountains to sandy deserts and *volcanic* islands.

WASHINGTON
▲ Mount Rainier

MONTANA

ROCKY MOUNTAINS

CASCADE RANGE

Columbia River

OREGON

IDAHO

Yellowstone National Park

UNITED STATES OF AMERICA

▲ Mount Shasta

CALIFORNIA

GREAT BASIN

Great Salt Lake

NEVADA

UTAH

WELCOME TO Fabulous LAS VEGAS NEVADA

COAST RANGES

SIERRA NEVADA

DEATH VALLEY
▲ Mount Whitney

Colorado River

ARIZONA

Mojave Desert

PACIFIC OCEAN

Sonoran Desert

HAWAII

Plants and animals

Black swallowtail butterfly

Bald eagle

Cougar

Redwood tree

Rocky Mountain goat

Giant saguaro cacti grow in the Sonoran Desert. They can grow to more than 43 feet (13 meters) tall.

People and places

Old Faithful Geyser

Cowboys

Mount Rushmore

Grand Canyon

Native Americans

Hollywood in California is well known for its *movie studios* and famous actors.

Missouri River

NORTH DAKOTA

SOUTH DAKOTA

WYOMING

NEBRASKA

▲ Mount Elbert
COLORADO

KANSAS

OKLAHOMA

NEW MEXICO

TEXAS

G R E A T   P L A I N S

ROCKY MOUNTAINS

Produce and resources

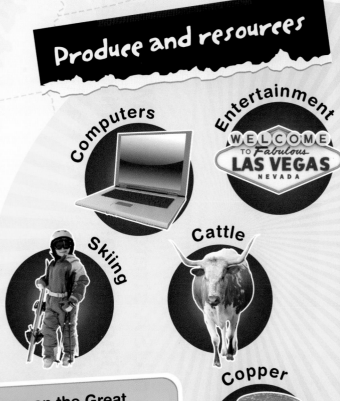

Computers

Entertainment

WELCOME TO *Fabulous* LAS VEGAS NEVADA

Skiing

Cattle

Copper

Farms on the Great Plains grow more **wheat** than anywhere else in the world.

People and places

Sears Tower

Football

Appalachian Mountains

Statue of Liberty

Cape Canaveral

Eastern USA

Eastern USA stretches from Minnesota to Florida. The capital of the United States, Washington D.C., is in the east.

The White House in Washington D.C. is the home of the President of the USA.

MAINE

VERMONT

NEW HAMPSHIRE

MASSACHUSETTS

RHODE ISLAND

CONNECTICUT

NEW JERSEY

NEW YORK

Lake Ontario

PENNSYLVANIA

MARYLAND

Washington D.C.

DELAWARE

WEST VIRGINIA

Ohio River

Lake Erie

OHIO

Lake Huron

MICHIGAN

INDIANA

Lake Superior

Lake Michigan

WISCONSIN

ILLINOIS

IOWA

MINNESOTA

Missouri River

U N I T E D   S T A T E S   O F   A M E R I C A

A P P A L A C H I A N   M O U N T A I N S

ATLANTIC OCEAN

Oranges

Jazz

Cars

steel

Pigs

The USA is one of the biggest cotton growers in the world.

VIRGINIA

NORTH CAROLINA

▲ Mount Mitchell

SOUTH CAROLINA

A P P A L A C H I A

GEORGIA

FLORIDA

MISSOURI

KENTUCKY

TENNESSEE

ALABAMA

ARKANSAS

MISSISSIPPI

LOUISIANA

Mississippi River

GULF OF MEXICO

Plants and animals

Florida manatee

prairie dog

Alligator

Lobster

Palmetto tree

Each year, millions of monarch butterflies fly from northern USA to Mexico.

North America

13

Mexico and Central America

Sonoran Desert

GULF OF CALIFORNIA

BAJA CALIFORNIA

SIERRA MADRE OCCIDENTAL

Rio Grande

SIERRA MADRE ORIENTAL

MEXICO

GULF OF MEXICO

Lake Chapala

Mexico City

▲ Pico de Orizaba

YUCATÁN PENINSULA

BELIZE

Belmopan

GUATEMALA

PACIFIC OCEAN

Guatemala City ●

San Salvador ●

EL SALVADOR

HONDURAS

Tegucigalpa

Managua

Central America is a strip of land linking the continents of North and South America. Mexico lies to the north of Central America, while the Caribbean Islands lie to the east.

Plants and animals

Prickly pear cactus

Toucan

Cuban Trogon

Scarlet ibis

Rain forest

Howler monkeys live in the Yucatán Peninsula in Mexico.

14

Panama Canal

Tikal Ruins

Colima Volcano

Kuna people

Rio Grande River

ATLANTIC OCEAN

Mexico City is the capital of Mexico. It is one of the biggest cities in the world.

BAHAMAS

● Nassau

TURKS AND CAICOS ISLANDS

VIRGIN ISLANDS   ANGUILLA   ST. MARTIN
ST. BARTHÉLEMY
SABA   ANTIGUA AND BARBUDA
PUERTO RICO   ST. EUSTATIUS   Basseterre   ● St. John's
ST. KITTS AND NEVIS   GUADELOUPE
DOMINICA
Roseau ●
MONTSERRAT   MARTINIQUE
Castries ●   BARBADOS
ST. LUCIA
Kingstown ●   Bridgetown
ST. VINCENT AND
GRENADA   THE GRENADINES
St George's ●

● Havana

CUBA

DOMINICAN REPUBLIC

HAITI
Port-au-Prince ●   Santo Domingo

CAYMAN ISLANDS

JAMAICA   ●
Kingston

CARIBBEAN SEA

CURAÇAO
ARUBA   BONAIRE

TRINIDAD AND TOBAGO
Port-of-Spain ●

NICARAGUA

COSTA RICA
San José

● Panama City

PANAMA

Sugar cane

Silver

Bananas

Textiles, or fabrics, made in Central America can be very brightly colored.

Coffee

Cricket

North America

15

16

Amazon River

Itaipu Dam

Brasília Cathedral

Kayapo people

Carnival

Angel Falls in Venezuela is the world's highest waterfall. It is 3,212 feet (979 meters) high.

Brazil and its neighbors

Brazil is the largest country in South America. It also has the biggest *population.* Many different languages are spoken in South America, such as Spanish, Portuguese, English, and Dutch.

ATLANTIC OCEAN

Lake Maracaibo

Caracas

VENEZUELA

Angel Falls

GUIANA HIGHLANDS

Orinoco River

Georgetown

Paramaribo

GUYANA

SURINAME

FRENCH GUIANA

Negro River

Amazon River

AMAZON BASIN

B R A Z I L

● Brasilia

M A T O G R O S S O

Paraná River

PARAGUAY

Asunción ●

URUGUAY

Montevideo ●

B R A Z I L I A N H I G H L A N D S

▲ Sugar Loaf Mountain

Cotton

Soybeans

Lumber

soccer

Wool

Brazil nuts, fruit, and rubber come from the Amazon rain forest.

Plants and animals

Jaguar

Scarlet macaw

Rubber tree

Giant water lily

Piranha

Rare golden lion tamarin monkeys live in an area of forest on Brazil's east coast.

South America

17

Along the Andes

The Andes Mountains stretch the length of South America. They run from Colombia in the north to Chile in the south.

Gauchos

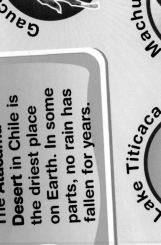
Machu Picchu

Moreno Glacier

Cotopaxi Volcano

Lake Titicaca

The Atacama Desert in Chile is the driest place on Earth. In some parts, no rain has fallen for years.

Pico Cristóbal Colón ▲

Bogotá
COLOMBIA

Quito
ECUADOR

Amazon River

PERU

▲ Huascarán
• Lima

ANDES MOUNTAINS

BOLIVIA

Lake Titicaca

GALÁPAGOS ISLANDS

Produce and resources

Emeralds

Coffee

Sheep

Copper

Sardines

Grapes are grown in *vineyards* in Chile. Most of them are used to make wine.

PACIFIC OCEAN

Paraná River

ANDES MOUNTAINS

Atacama Desert

CHILE

Valparaíso
Santiago

Cerro Aconcagua

ARGENTINA

Buenos Aires

PATAGONIA

FALKLAND ISLANDS

Tierra del Fuego

Cape Horn

Plants and animals

Mangrove swamp

Spectacled bear

Magellan penguin

Andean tapir

Andean condor

People living in the Andes keep llamas for carrying goods and for meat, milk, and wool.

North Africa and the Sahara

Parts of north Africa are covered by the Sahara Desert, the largest desert in the world. Many **coastal** areas have less dry weather, so **crops** can grow well.

ATLANTIC OCEAN

Strait of Gibraltar

•Algiers   •Tunis

CEUTA   MELILLA

MADEIRA

Rabat•

MOROCCO   ATLAS MOUNTAINS   **TUNISIA**   MEDITERRANEAN SEA

Mount Toubkal▲   Tripoli•

CANARY ISLANDS   •Surt

ALGERIA   LIBYA

S a h a r a   D e s e r t   Libyan

WESTERN SAHARA

AHAGGAR MOUNTAINS

MAURITANIA

Nouakchott•

Plants and animals

Tamarind tree

Nile crocodile

Camel

Gelada

Scorpion

The **fennec fox's** large ears keep it cool by letting heat escape from its body.

Sand dunes

Leptis Magna ruins

Berber people

Red Sea

Mosque

The **pyramids** in Egypt were built thousands of years ago as *tombs* for kings.

Produce and resources

Fish

Cotton

Sorghum

Coffee

Carpets

Suez Canal

Cairo

Sinai Peninsula

EGYPT

Nile River

Nubian Desert

RED SEA

ERITREA
Khartoum
Asmara

Ras Dashen ▲

Lake Tana

GULF OF ADEN

DJIBOUTI
Djibouti

SUDAN

Blue Nile River

Addis Ababa

SOMALIA

White Nile River

ETHIOPIA

INDIAN OCEAN

Mogadishu

Dates grow on date palms. They are found all over North Africa.

West, central, and east Africa

West, central, and east Africa stretches from Senegal in the west to Kenya in the east. In the west and center are **rain forests**. In the north and east are **grasslands**.

MALI

S a h a r a   D e s e r t

Niger River

NIGER

CAPE VERDE

● Praia

Dakar ● **SENEGAL**

Banjul ● **GAMBIA**

Niamey ●

Lake
Chad

ATLANTIC
OCEAN

Bissau ●
**GUINEA-
BISSAU**

GUINEA

Bamako ●

Ouagadougou ●

BURKINA FASO

N'Djamena

NIGERIA

Conakry ●

BENIN

Freetown ●
SIERRA LEONE

**IVORY
COAST**

*Lake
Volta* **TOGO**

Abuja ●

Monrovia ●

Yamoussoukro ●

GHANA

Porto-
Novo ●

LIBERIA Abidjan ●

Lomé ●
Accra ●

Cotonou ●

CAMEROON

GULF OF
GUINEA

Malabo ●

● Yaoundé

EQUATORIAL GUINEA

São Tomé ●

● Libreville

**SÃO TOMÉ
AND PRÍNCIPE**

GABON

**REPUBLIC O
THE CONGO**

Brazzaville ●
Kinshasa ●

Plants and animals

Acacia tree

Hippopotamus

Elephant

Flamingo

Sand viper

Mountain gorillas live in the Volcanoes National Park in Rwanda. Only a few hundred of them are left.

People and places

Tuareg people

Maasai people

Niger River

Sahara Desert

Dakar

Mount Kilimanjaro is the tallest mountain in Africa. It is more than 19,330 feet (5,890 meters) high.

Produce and resources

Palm oil

Diamonds

Cocoa

Cashew nuts

Cattle

Cassava root is one of the most widely eaten foods in Africa.

CHAD

CENTRAL AFRICAN REPUBLIC

Bangui

Congo River

DEMOCRATIC REPUBLIC OF THE CONGO

RWANDA   Kigali

Bujumbura

BURUNDI

Lake Tanganyika

UGANDA

Kampala

Lake Victoria

Lake Turkana

GREAT RIFT VALLEY

KENYA

▲Mount Kenya

Nairobi

▲Mount Kilimanjaro

Dodoma

Dar es Salaam

TANZANIA

Southern Africa

Hot, dry deserts stretch across large areas of southern Africa. The island of Madagascar lies to the east. Lots of amazing *wildlife* lives there.

ATLANTIC OCEAN

Luanda

ANGOLA

ZAMBIA

Lusaka

Victoria Falls

Namib

NAMIBIA

Okavango Delta

Windhoek

BOTSWANA

Kalahari Desert

Gaborone

Pretoria

Desert

Orange River

Maseru

LESOTHO

SOUTH AFRICA

Table Mountain

Cape Town

Cape of Good Hope

Plants and animals

Leopard tortoise

Springbok

Baobab tree

Dwarf chameleon

Zebra

Lemurs are monkey-like animals that live on the island of Madagascar.

People and places

Victoria Falls

Zulu people

Cape of Good Hope

Table Mountain has a very flat top. It is just outside Cape Town in South Africa.

Kalahari Desert

San people

● Victoria

SEYCHELLES

● Moroni

COMOROS MAYOTTE

INDIAN OCEAN

Lake Malawi

● Lilongwe
MALAWI

Zambezi River

● Harare
ZIMBABWE

MOZAMBIQUE CHANNEL

MADAGASCAR

● Antananarivo

MAURITIUS
● Port Louis

REUNION

MOZAMBIQUE

Limpopo River

● Maputo
Mbabane
Lobamba
WAZILAND

Produce and resources

Shellfish

Grapes

Cloves

Maize

Sugar cane

Tourism is a large business in southern Africa. People travel here to go on *safari*.

Northern Europe

Northern Europe stretches from the Republic of Ireland in the west to Latvia in the east. Northern parts such as Norway and Sweden can be very cold. Thick forests grow in some of these countries.

ICELAND
●Reykjavik

Plants and animals

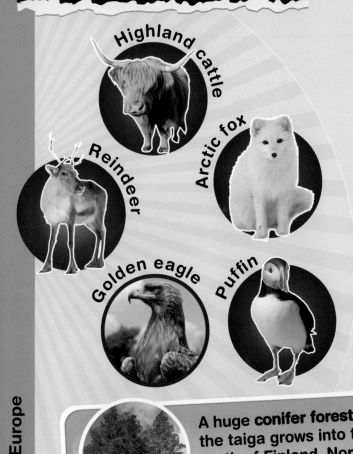

Highland cattle

Reindeer

Arctic fox

Golden eagle

Puffin

THE FAEROES

SHETLAND ISLANDS

ATLANTIC OCEAN

OUTER HEBRIDES

ORKNEY ISLANDS

SCOTLAND

GRAMPIAN MOUNTAINS
▲Ben Nevis
Forth River

NORTH SEA

NORTHERN IRELAND

REPUBLIC OF IRELAND
Dublin ●

ISLE OF MAN

ENGLAND

UNITED KINGDOM

Mount Snowdon ▲

IRISH SEA

Severn River

WALES

Thames River
● London

A huge **conifer forest** called the taiga grows into the north of Finland, Norway, and Sweden.

ISLES OF SCILLY

ENGLISH CHANNEL

JERSEY

GUERNSEY

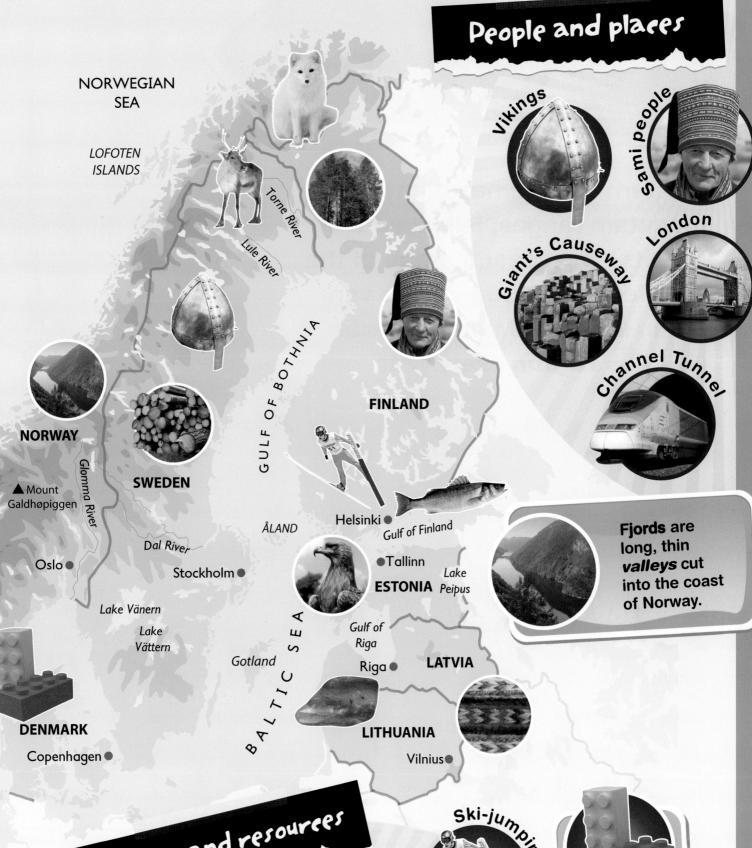

NORWEGIAN SEA

LOFOTEN ISLANDS

Torne River

Lule River

GULF OF BOTHNIA

FINLAND

NORWAY

▲ Mount Galdhøpiggen

Glomma River

SWEDEN

Dal River

Oslo ●

Stockholm ●

Helsinki ●

Gulf of Finland

ÅLAND

Lake Vänern

Lake Vättern

● Tallinn

ESTONIA

Lake Peipus

Gotland

Gulf of Riga

Riga ●

LATVIA

B A L T I C   S E A

LITHUANIA

Vilnius ●

DENMARK

Copenhagen ●

Vikings

Sami people

Giant's Causeway

London

Channel Tunnel

Fjords are long, thin **valleys** cut into the coast of Norway.

Produce and resources

Ski-jumping

Lumber

Textiles

Sea bass

Amber

The **Legoland®** theme park in Denmark is built from 50 million Lego bricks.

Western Europe

Western Europe has many mountain ranges, lakes, and forests. The coastal areas of the Mediterranean Sea can be very hot in summer. Many **tourists** visit this **region** every year.

ENGLISH CHANNEL

Paris •

Loire River

FRANCE

BAY OF BISCAY

ATLANTIC OCEAN

MASSIF CENTRAL

PYRENEES MOUNTAINS

IBERIAN MOUNTAINS

Ebro River

ANDORRA Andorra la Vella

SPAIN

Madrid •

PORTUGAL

Tagus River

Lisbon •

BALEARIC ISLANDS

Guadalquivir River

GIBRALTAR
CEUTA

MELILLA

Plants and animals

Hoopoe

Red deer

Mountain goat

Wild horse

Pine tree

Alpine marmots spend the winter fast asleep in **burrows**, or dens, underneath the ground.

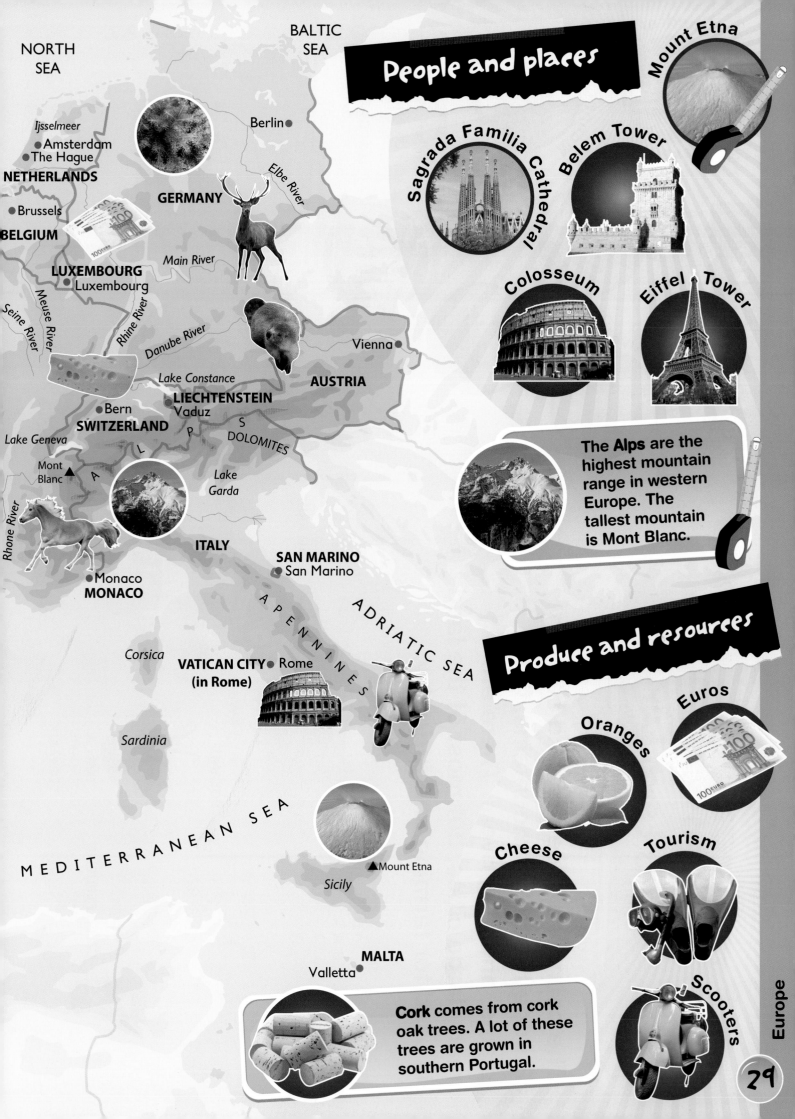

NORTH SEA

BALTIC SEA

People and places

Mount Etna

Sagrada Familia Cathedral

Belem Tower

Colosseum

Eiffel Tower

Ijsselmeer
Amsterdam
The Hague
NETHERLANDS

Berlin

GERMANY

Elbe River

Brussels
BELGIUM

Main River

LUXEMBOURG
Luxembourg

Meuse River

Rhine River

Danube River

Seine River

Lake Constance

Bern
SWITZERLAND

LIECHTENSTEIN
Vaduz

Vienna

AUSTRIA

Lake Geneva

Mont Blanc

A L P S

DOLOMITES

Lake Garda

The **Alps** are the highest mountain range in western Europe. The tallest mountain is Mont Blanc.

Rhone River

ITALY

Monaco
MONACO

SAN MARINO
San Marino

A P E N N I N E S

ADRIATIC SEA

Produce and resources

Corsica

VATICAN CITY
(in Rome)

Rome

Sardinia

M E D I T E R R A N E A N   S E A

▲Mount Etna

Sicily

Oranges

Euros

Cheese

Tourism

MALTA
Valletta

Scooters

Cork comes from cork oak trees. A lot of these trees are grown in southern Portugal.

Central and eastern Europe

The countries of central and eastern Europe have high mountains, flat plains, and long rivers. There are many large cities, but most of the land is used for farming and *industry*.

People and places

Alexander Nevsky Cathedral

Mount Olympus

Peles Castle

Vistula River

Kiev

The Parthenon stands on a hill in Athens in Greece. It is almost 2,500 years old.

BALTIC SEA

CZECH REPUBLIC
• Prague

Oder River

POLAND
• Warsaw

SLOVAKIA
• Bratislava

TATRA ▲ Mount Gerlach
MOUNTAINS

BELARUS
• Minsk

Vistula River

CARPATHIAN MOUNTAINS

UKRAINE
• Kiev

Dnieper River

MOLDOVA
Chisinau •

SEA OF AZOV

Crimea

BLACK SEA

Produce and resources

Olive oil

Glass

Cattle

Machinery

Tourism

The roses that grow in Bulgaria are a special type that can be used to make a scented oil.

SLOVENIA
Ljubljana

HUNGARY
Zagreb

CROATIA

BOSNIA AND
HERZEGOVINA
Sarajevo

OMANIA

Bucharest
Danube River

BALKAN MOUNTAINS

Sofia

BULGARIA

Belgrade

SERBIA

Pristina

KOSOVO

Skopje

MACEDONIA

MONTENEGRO
Podgorica

Tirane
ALBANIA

PINDUS MOUNTAINS

Mount
Olympus
GREECE

Athens

AEGEAN SEA

SEA OF CRETE

Crete

MEDITERRANEAN SEA

ADRIATIC SEA

Dolphins can be seen swimming next to boats in the Aegean Sea.

Plants and animals

Grey wolf

Conifer trees

Chamois

Edelweiss

Pelican

Europe

31

ARCTIC OCEAN

Russia is the biggest country in the world. It stretches across the two continents of Europe and Asia. The eight countries of central Asia lie to the southwest of Russia.

BARENTS SEA

RUSSIA

Moscow

URAL MOUNTAINS

R U S

Ob River

Volga River

BLACK SEA

Mount Elbrus▲

E

S   T   E   P   P

GEORGIA

Tbilisi

ARMENIA
Yerevan

CASPIAN
SEA

Aral
Sea

Astana

KAZAKHSTAN

Lake Balkhash

AZERBAIJAN

Baku

Amu Darya River

UZBEKISTAN

TURKMENISTAN

Tashkent

Bishkek

KYRGYZSTAN

Ashgabat

Dushanbe

TAJIKISTAN

Plants and animals

Harp seal

Brown bear

Taiga forest

Elk

Wild mushroom

The **Siberian tiger** only lives in the far east of Russia, on the border with China.

BERING
SEA

Volga River

Space Center

SIBERIA

Saint Basil's Cathedral

Lake Baikal

SEA OF OKHOTSK

Mount Elbrus

S I B E R I A

I A

Lena River

Lake Baikal

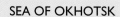

The **Nenet people** live in northern Russia. They make clothes from animal skin to keep warm.

PACIFIC OCEAN

Grain

Bolshoi Ballet

Caviar

Coal

Oil

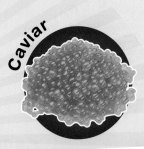

The **Trans-Siberian Railway** runs from eastern Europe to China.

Europe

33

Middle East

BLACK SEA

Sea of Marmara

Mount Ararat ▲

• Ankara
TURKEY

AEGEAN SEA

ANATOLIAN PLATEAU

Lake Van

Lake Urmia

TAURUS MOUNTAINS

Tigris River

Lake Assad

Euphrates River

SYRIA

Baghdad •

Most of the Middle East is covered with hot, sandy deserts. In some countries, huge amounts of *oil* have been found underneath the deserts.

CYPRUS • Nicosia

MEDITERRANEAN SEA

LEBANON
Beirut •

Syrian Desert

• Damascus

IRAQ

ISRAEL

WEST BANK
• Amman

Jerusalem •
GAZA STRIP Dead Sea

JORDAN

Arabian

RED SEA

Plants and animals

Dung beetle

Flamingo

Moray eel

Tulip

Camel

The **Arabian oryx** lives in the Arabian Desert. It can go for weeks without drinking water.

Burj-Al-Arab Hotel

Petra ruins

Kaaba building

Mount Ararat

Blue Mosque

The **Dead Sea** is a lake between Israel and Jordan. It is so salty, you can float in the water.

CASPIAN SEA

▲ Mount Demavend
● Tehran

Kavir Desert

IRAN

Lut Desert

ZAGROS MOUNTAINS

KUWAIT
● Kuwait City

BAHRAIN
Manama ●   QATAR
● Doha

● Abu Dhabi

UNITED ARAB EMIRATES   OMAN

GULF OF OMAN

● Muscat

ARABIAN SEA

● Riyadh

SAUDI ARABIA

Rub 'al Khali (Empty Quarter)

Desert

YEMEN

● Sanaa

Sheep

Wheat

Dates

Coffee

Tea

Iran is famous for its handmade Persian **carpets**. They are made of wool.

Asia

35

People and places

Southern Asia

Mount Everest

Drupka people

Sri Meenakshi Temple

Thar Desert

Ganges River

The Taj Mahal in India was built as a tomb for an Indian *empress* more than 400 years ago.

AFGHANISTAN

Kabul

Islamabad

PAKISTAN

Indus River

Thar Desert

Delhi

Narmada River

NEPAL

Kathmandu

H   I   M   A   L   A   Y   A   S

Mount Everest

Ganges River

BHUTAN

Thimphu

BANGLADESH

Dhaka

INDIA

BAY OF BENGAL

India is the largest country in southern Asia. Mount Everest, the highest mountain in the world, is in the Himalayas, to the north east of India.

ANDAMAN
ISLANDS

NICOBAR
ISLANDS

Produce and resources

Tourism

Nuts

Tea

Rice

Leather

Sri Lanka is famous for gemstones, including sapphires, amethysts, and rubies.

INDIAN OCEAN

EASTERN GHATS

SRI LANKA

Colombo ●

WESTERN GHATS

ARABIAN
SEA

● Malé

MALDIVES

The snow leopard's thick fur coat keeps it warm in its cold mountain home.

Plants and animals

Tiger

Elephant

Peacock

Lotus flower

Red panda

South East Asia

South East Asia is a hot, rainy area, made up of a small piece of **mainland** and many small islands. The country of Indonesia alone has more than 3,000 islands.

Hkakabo Razi

Irrawaddy River

Salween River

BURMA

Naypyidaw

VIETNAM •Hanoi

LAOS

•Vientiane

Mekong River

SOUTH CHINA SEA

THAILAND

Bangkok

ANDAMAN SEA

CAMBODIA

Phnom Penh

M A L A Y S I A

•Kuala Lumpur
Putrajaya   **SINGAPORE**
•Singapore

BARISAN MOUNTAINS

Sumatra

INDIAN OCEAN

JAVA SEA

Anak Krakatoa ▲   •Jakarta   Java

Plants and animals

Rafflesia flower

Tapir

Flying fox

Orangutan

Hornbill

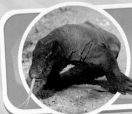

The **Komodo dragon** of Indonesia grows up to 10 feet (3 meters) long. It is the world's largest lizard.

People and places

Asmat people

Mekong River

Mount Pinatubo

Petronas Towers

Borobodur monument

Luzon

▲ Mount Pinatubo

● Manila

PHILIPPINES

PACIFIC OCEAN

Angkor Wat is a *temple* in Cambodia. It was built many hundreds of years ago.

Palawan

Mindanao

SULU SEA

CELEBES SEA

MALUKU ISLANDS

Western New Guinea

Puncak Jaya ▲

● Bandar Seri Begawan

BRUNEI

SERAM SEA

Seram

ARU ISLANDS

Borneo

Sulawesi

BANDA SEA

I N D O N E S I A

FLORES SEA

● Dili

EAST TIMOR

Flores

Lombok

Bali

SUMBA

Produce and resources

Coconuts

Sandalwood

Rubies

Tin

Rubber

The Maluku Islands are famous for growing cinnamon, nutmeg, and other **spices**.

China and its neighbors

China and its **neighboring** countries lie in the eastern part of Asia. China is an enormous country—one in every five people in the world live there.

ALTAI MOUNTAINS

Ulaanbaatar ●

MONGOLIA

Gobi Desert

Huang He River

Taklimakan Desert

ALTUN MOUNTAINS

KUNLUN MOUNTAINS

KARAKORAM MOUNTAINS

HIMALAYAS

C H I N A

PLATEAU OF TIBET

Yangtze River

▲ Mount Everest

Plants and animals

Dhole wild dog

Macaque monkey

Yak

Japanese cormorant

Orchid

Giant pandas only live in a few mountain forests in China where they feed on **bamboo**.

Terracotta Army

Hong Kong

Gobi Desert

Grand Canal

Mount Fuji

Hokkaido

SEA OF JAPAN

Honshu

JAPAN

Tokyo

Mount Fuji ▲

NORTH KOREA

●Pyongyang

●Seoul

SOUTH KOREA

Shikoku

Korea Strait

YELLOW SEA

Kyushu

PACIFIC OCEAN

EAST CHINA SEA

Beijing ●

Grand Canal

●Taipei

TAIWAN

HONG KONG MACAO

SOUTH CHINA SEA

Hainan

The **Great Wall of China** runs for almost 2,175 miles (3,500 kilometers) across China.

Computers

Televisions

Ships

Banks

Rice

Fish is a very popular food in Japan. More fish is caught here than in any other country.

Australia

Australia is one of the biggest countries in the world. The neighboring country of New Zealand is made up of two smaller islands. In the Pacific Ocean nearby are hundreds of islands.

PAPUA NEW GUINEA

Mount Hagen

Port Moresby ●

CORAL SEA

INDIAN OCEAN

Great Sandy Desert

NORTHERN TERRITORY

QUEENSLAND

AUSTRALIA

WESTERN AUSTRALIA

Simpson Desert

GREAT DIVIDING RANGE

Great Victoria Desert

SOUTH AUSTRALIA

Lake Eyre

NEW SOUTH WALES

● Canberra
AUSTRALIAN CAPITAL TERRITORY

VICTORIA

Bass Strait

Tasmania

Plants and animals

Coconut palm tree

Kiwi bird

Crocodile

Eucalyptus tree

Humpback whale

Kangaroos are animals called *marsupials*. Mothers carry their baby in a *pouch*.

People and places

Sydney Opera House

Aborigine people

Ayers Rock

Maori people

Lake Eyre

PACIFIC OCEAN

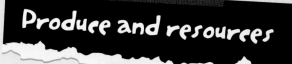
The **Great Barrier Reef** off eastern Australia is the longest *coral reef* in the world.

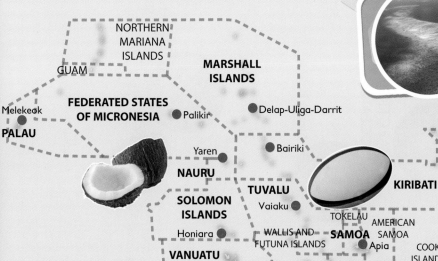

NORTHERN
MARIANA
ISLANDS

GUAM

MARSHALL
ISLANDS

Melekeok
PALAU

FEDERATED STATES
OF MICRONESIA   • Palikir

Delap-Uliga-Darrit

Yaren
NAURU

• Bairiki

KIRIBATI

TUVALU
Vaiaku

SOLOMON
ISLANDS

TOKELAU

AMERICAN
SAMOA

Honiara

WALLIS AND
FUTUNA ISLANDS

SAMOA
• Apia

COOK
ISLANDS

VANUATU

• Vila

Suva

NIUE

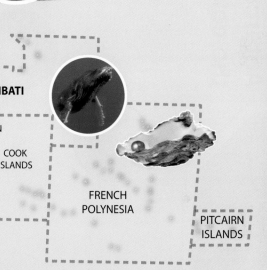

NEW
CALEDONIA

FIJI

TONGA
• Nuku'alofa

FRENCH
POLYNESIA

PITCAIRN
ISLANDS

North Island
Cook Strait
• Wellington
NEW ZEALAND
SOUTHERN ▲ Mount Cook
ALPS   South Island

Produce and resources

Wool

Black pearls

Rugby

Opals
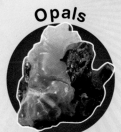

Sweet potatoes

New Zealand grows more **kiwi fruit** than anywhere else in the world.

Australia

43

The Arctic and Antarctica

The Arctic is in the north of the world. Antarctica is in the south. They are the coldest places on Earth.

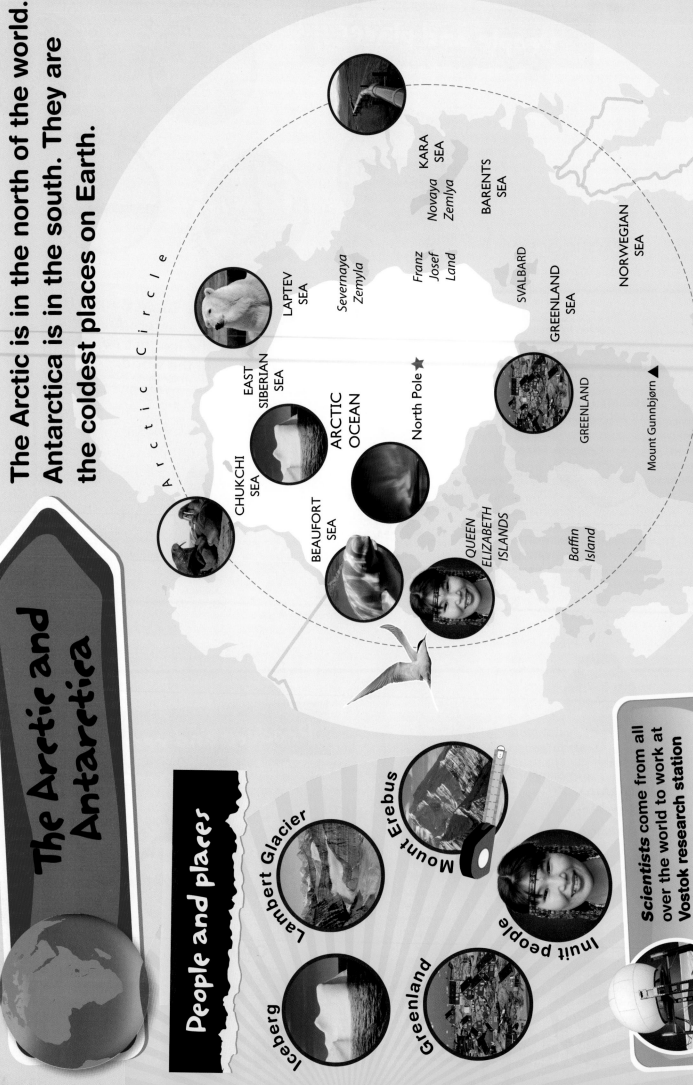

Arctic Circle

KARA SEA

Novaya Zemlya

BARENTS SEA

Franz Josef Land

Severnaya Zemyla

SVALBARD

NORWEGIAN SEA

GREENLAND SEA

LAPTEV SEA

EAST SIBERIAN SEA

North Pole ★

ARCTIC OCEAN

GREENLAND

Mount Gunnbjørn ▲

CHUKCHI SEA

BEAUFORT SEA

QUEEN ELIZABETH ISLANDS

Baffin Island

People and places

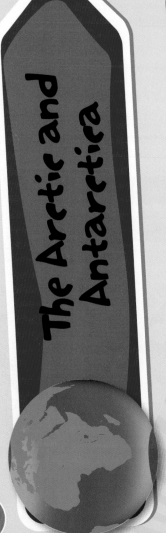

Iceberg

Greenland

Lambert Glacier

Mount Erebus

Inuit people

Scientists come from all over the world to work at Vostok research station in Antarctica.

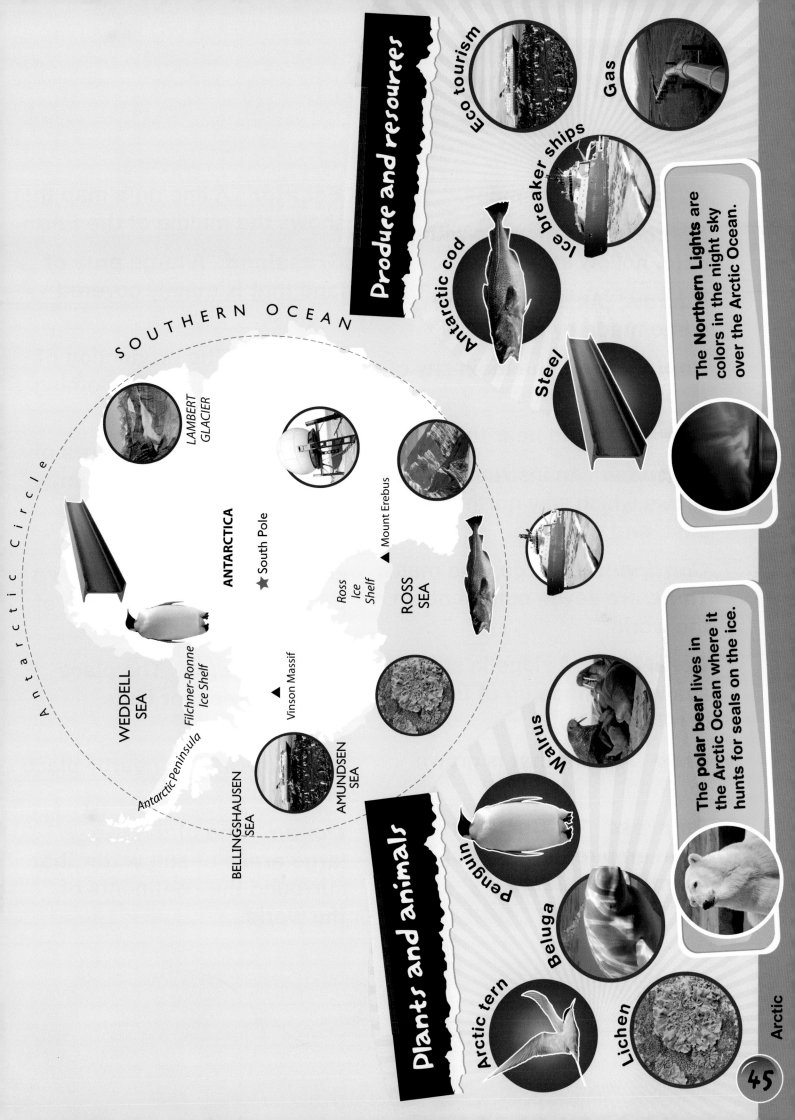

Produce and resources

Eco tourism

Gas

Ice breaker ships

Antarctic cod

Steel

The Northern Lights are colors in the night sky over the Arctic Ocean.

SOUTHERN OCEAN

Antarctic Circle

LAMBERT GLACIER

ANTARCTICA

★ South Pole

▲ Mount Erebus

Ross Ice Shelf

ROSS SEA

WEDDELL SEA

Filchner-Ronne Ice Shelf

Vinson Massif ▲

Antarctic Peninsula

BELLINGSHAUSEN SEA

AMUNDSEN SEA

The polar bear lives in the Arctic Ocean where it hunts for seals on the ice.

Walrus

Plants and animals

Penguin

Beluga

Arctic tern

Lichen

45

Glossary

Atlas A book of maps.

Bamboo A tall grass with hard, hollow stems.

Burrow An underground home made by an animal.

Capital city The main city of a country or state.

Coastal Land near the sea.

Compass An instrument that shows which way north, south, east, and west are.

Continent A large land mass. There are seven continents in the world.

Coral reef A ridge in shallow sea water made up of tiny coral animals.

Crop A plant that is grown for food.

Empress The female ruler of an empire, or group of countries or states.

Equator A line on a map that shows the middle of the Earth.

Grassland A large area of land that is mainly covered in grass.

Industry The production of a large amount of something, such as machinery.

Mainland The main area of land that makes up a country or continent.

Marsupial An animal that carries its babies around in a pocket of skin on the front of its body.

Movie studios The place where movies, or films, are made.

Neighboring A nearby place or country.

Ocean One of the five large areas of salt water that surround the continents of the world.

Oil   A liquid that is used to make machines, such as cars, work.

Pod   A group of animals in the sea that live together.

Population   The number of people living in a certain area, city, or country.

Pouch   A pocket of skin on the front of a marsupial's body that is used to carry its baby.

Rain forest   A tropical area that has lots of trees that grow closely together.

Region   A large area of a country.

Rink   A surface of ice made for ice skating or ice hockey.

Safari   A special trip to see wild animals, normally in Africa.

Scale   A way of measuring the size of something, for example, a mountain.

Scented oil   An oil made from something with a pleasant smell, such as roses.

Scientist   A person who studies sciences such as chemistry, physics, and biology to learn about the world around us.

Symbol   A picture or sign that has a particular meaning.

Temple   A building where people go to pray.

Textiles   Woven cloth that is made in large amounts.

Tomb   A place where a dead person is buried.

Tourist   Someone who is visiting a country or place for pleasure.

Valley   A low area of land that sits between two higher areas of land.

Vineyard   Land where grapes are grown.

Volcanic   The land, ash, or lava that is related to a volcano. For example, Hawaii is made up of volcanic islands.

Wildlife   Animals and plants.

Index